DAVID DEL TREDICI

LAMENT FOR THE DEATH OF A BULLFIGHTER

A cycle of nine songs to a poem by Joshua Beckman

for Soprano and Piano

BOOSEY & HAWKES

DISTRIBUTED BY

HAL•LEONARD®
CORPORATION

7777 W. BLUEMOUND RD. P.O. BOX 13819 MILWAUKEE, WI 53213

www.boosey.com
www.halleonard.com

COMPOSER'S NOTE

One evening in 1995, at the Virginia Center for the Creative Arts, I heard the young poet Joshua Beckman read his *Lament*. Before long I was crying, and it became clear to me that I would one day set his poem to music. Was it because I had just lost a lover to AIDS? Whatever the trigger, Beckman had touched that deep place where music longs to connect with words and to trap forever (or so composers hope) the heart's tremulous, fleeting emotion.

Beckman begins all nine sections of the poem with the same line—"At the news of your death." Each goes on to describe the repercussions of this "news" throughout the world. It is a startling vision: "Children could hold back their giggling no more," "a giant wave finally reached our country and sat his gray body down," "the computers… went on strike and had to be replaced with people," "not a good poem was written… not by any of the famous poets from anywhere," "every dinner, no matter curried or cajun,... came out sweeter, unbelievably sweeter," "the trees became sad... and they decided to skip summer." In this blend of whimsy, humor and innocent wonder, sadness enters only occasionally, as if by accident. Yet feelings of loss, like tiny droplets do gradually accumulate. By the end, this oddly touching, poetic landscape seems almost to tremble, suffused as it is now by the poet's moist, heartfelt tears.

The nine sections of the poem are connected, each to the next, by music (the only exception being between the first and second songs). To mirror Beckman's repeated use of the same first line, I repeat the theme of the first song in each song that follows, though not necessarily at the beginning.

I have added titles to each of the nine sections and have reversed the order of the texts for the seventh and eighth songs.

The cycle was written in 1998 at both the MacDowell Colony and Yaddo, then revised and expanded in 2001 at the Rockefeller Foundation's Study Center in Bellagio, Italy.

Children (*dedicated to Joanna Lee*)
The cycle opens with the filigreed theme that will be heard in each of the subsequent songs. Here, the theme is harmonized in four different ways leading to a contrasting section in the minor and to a surprisingly bi-tonal coda.

A Giant Wave (*dedicated to Stephen Burke*)
This fast boisterous song is, in the piano, a roiling sea of dotted rhythms and canonic imitation. The soprano rides this wave in *declamando* style.

A Few Romances (*dedicated to Tobias Schneebaum and Joel Singer*)
Beginning with a quiet reminiscence of *Children*, this song offers refuge from the storm immediately preceding. Only towards the end, in a piano solo connecting this song to the next, does the emotional temperature rise.

Walking (*dedicated to John "Matty" Krams*)
This short song, a chain of dominant seventh chords, walks along in a steadily moving quarter-note rhythm. Finally, it vanishes "and has not been heard from since," as the poem says.

Rebellion (*dedicated to John Corigliano*)
This dramatic, comic scene weaves together a conglomeration of Wagner and Strauss quotes. The vocal line is stratospheric— a veritable hanging garden of soprano tendrils.

A Good Cry (*dedicated to Tom Cipullo*)
An abrupt change of mood, this is the cycle's sad song. Because jazz and I have had little to do with each other, the "jazzy" feel of *A Good Cry*, especially in its middle section, comes as a surprise even to me.

A Point of Contention (*dedicated to my brothers—Bobby, Richard and Peter*)
Fast and angry, full of unrest and shifting harmonies, this song contains a *quodlibet* where its main theme is combined with the *idée fixe* theme of the first song.

Sweeter (*dedicated to my sister, Ann*)
This hushed, quiet song, *recitativo* in style, builds suspense for the aria that will come—but not right away. The intervening piano interlude is elaborate and virtuosic. The "falling octave" motive, which gains prominence as the motion subsides, anticipates the final song.

David (*dedicated to myself!*)
In a rocking lullaby tempo, this is more aria than song, rising to a grandly passionate climax amid swirls of trills. There is a "David" coda where the name, repeated five times, gradually dies away. The *Children* theme makes an appearance in its original form but quickly diminishes to the vanishing point. A glowing piano postlude closes the cycle in high Neo-romantic style.

—*David Del Tredici*

Commissioned by the Abby Whiteside Foundation

First performed December 4, 2001
at Weill Recital Hall in New York City, by
Hila Plitmann, soprano; David Del Tredici, piano

CONTENTS

Duration: *ca.* 45 min.

Vocal Texts

LAMENT FOR THE DEATH OF A BULLFIGHTER
by
Joshua Beckman

I. Children

At the news of your death
children could hold back their giggling no more
and fits of laughter spread like chickenpox
all over this country,
and at first no one noticed
because kids are always doing stuff like that,
but soon there was no stopping them
no quieting them down at all
and then the sky turned dark
and authority slunk away
like the man who never wanted to be sheriff
and the kids stayed outside
floating down the streets in boats made from junk
and when the moon showed up
they finally went in
left their soaking clothes at the door
and headed straight for their computers.
And then we had lost them to you
their eyes glued to the screen
their fragile hearts pumping with electric blood
and their thousand little thumbs
frantically bouncing up and down.

II. A Giant Wave

At the news of your death
pardon me, the mail is slow from there to here,
a giant wave finally reached our country
and sat his big gray body down
next to the few people left
who hadn't run away in fear
(again like the movies)
and the wave told such a captivating
transcontinental story that we didn't notice
him turning to mud like an ice cream cone
and when we looked, all that was left
were a dozen pie-shaped jellyfish,
but the ocean took those back quickly,
before any trouble got started.

III. A Few Romances

At the news of your death
the computers at the phone company
all over New York City
and the surrounding areas
went on strike
and had to be replaced
with people
who made every connection
and answered every question,
much to the surprise of the callers
who had become accustomed to automation
and no matter how many people called
(and once the lonely bachelors found out
there were a lot)
everything went smoothly as could be
due to the courtesy and stealth of those young operators
and although things got back to normal the next day
—no reflection on you—
more than a few romances
budded out of the sparks of that confusion.

IV. Walking

At the news of your death
couples who had never heard of you
kept walking
and were only dragged back
by the nagging sensation
that after hundreds of miles
they had left homes and families unattended.
And one source stated
that a woman in her early thirties
after returning and finding that she
had not left her oven on
headed directly back out
and has not been heard from since.

V. Rebellion

At the news of your death
in every hospital in America
and all at once
babies were born
and then slapped on the butt,
and preschoolers woke up early from their naps
and the more the teachers yelled
and snapped their red rulers
the more riled up the little ones became.
At home, all they would have for dinner
was chocolate milk
and they threw their pajamas out the window
and snuck dirty books to bed
and the next day everyone wore
their crusty fake mustaches to school
and answered their teacher's questions
in rhyme.

VI. A Good Cry

At the news of your death
not a good poem was written
not in your country or mine
not by any of the famous poets from anywhere,
no, we all just sat down and had a good cry,
even the ones who didn't think so much of you
got up from their chairs, misty,
thinking it was their wives or their age
or the millennium
and no matter what we did,
none of us could get back to it,
not for a good long while.

VII. A Point of Contention

At the news of your death
on the day that you died
the paper came with a little note
saying that you were a crazy and a good man,
which I knew
and that you were a talented poet
with thirty books to your credit,
which I knew
and saying that you were dead,
so I went out and threw it in the street.
Later the neighbors would mention it
and I would get sad, and wouldn't explain,
and I expect it will be a point of contention for a while.

VIII. Sweeter

At the news of your death
everyone turned on the tv
and left the room
at the news of your death
everyone took pictures
that would come out blurry
at the news of your death
every dinner, no matter curried or cajun,
came out sweeter, unbelievably sweeter
than anyone could have imagined.

(Piano Interlude)

IX. David

David, at the news of your death
the trees became sad,
not all of them of course,
but a few in every country,
and they decided to skip summer
and drop their leaves right then
and despite confusion on the ground,
birds in naked nests, and wind with nothing to do
all over the world they have proposed to keep this up.
You see, being trees they can't believe you're not coming back,
and they say that they will do this year after year,
stubborn and ignorant trees that they are,
they have promised to keep this up
despite official protests and calm pleading of every kind
they are determined to keep this up David.
Yes, they are determined to keep this up
until you return.

LAMENT FOR THE DEATH OF A BULLFIGHTER

for Joanna Lee

I. Children

JOSHUA BECKMAN

DAVID DEL TREDICI

Poco allegro (♩ = 116)

At the news of your death chil - dren could hold back their gig - gling no_____ more_____ and fits of laugh - ter spread like chick - en -

Text: © by Joshua Beckman
from THINGS ARE HAPPENING, APR

M-051-93368-6

Printed in U.S.A.

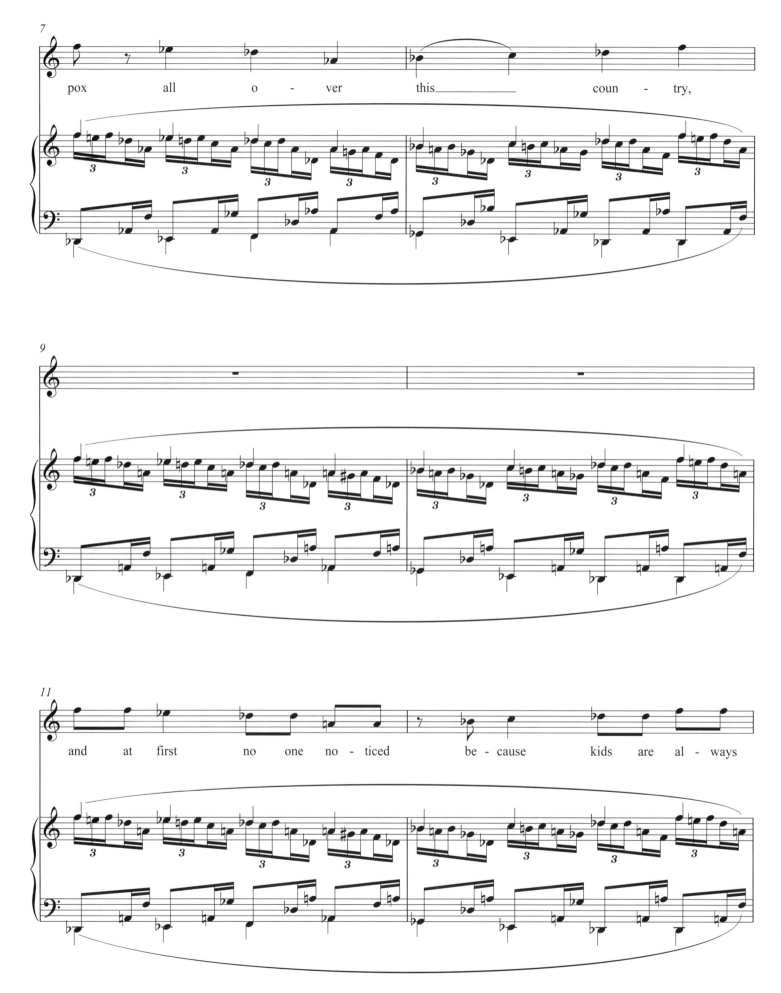

pox all o - ver this_____ coun - try,

and at first no one no - ticed be - cause kids are al - ways

do - ing stuff like that, but soon there was no stop - ping

them no qui - et - ing them down at_____ all_____

and then the sky turned dark___

___ and au - thor - i - ty slunk a - way

ritard.

like the man who nev - er want - ed to be___

6

thou - sand lit - tle thumbs fran - ti-c'lly bounc - ing up and down.

fran - ti - c'lly bounc - ing up and down.

fran - ti - c'lly bounc - ing up and down.

for Stephen Burke

II. A Giant Wave

JOSHUA BECKMAN

DAVID DEL TREDICI

Allegro con fuoco e marcato (♩ = 160)

N.B. Mark clearly the canon between right and left hands.

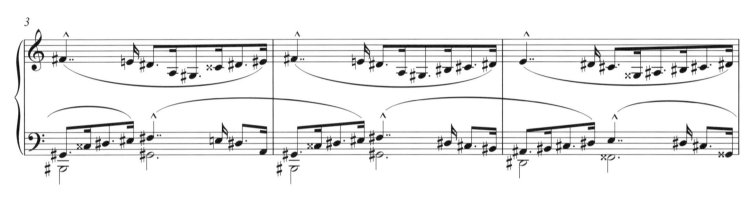

At the news of your death par - don me, the mail is

slow from there to here, a gi - ant wave fi - nal - ly reached our

coun - try and sat____ his big grey bo - dy down next to the

few peo - ple left__ who__ had - n't run a - way in fear

16

were a doz - en pie - shaped jel - ly - fish,

but_____ the o - - - cean

took_____ those back_____ quick - - ly,

Passionato

be - fore an - y trou - ble

got_____ start - ed. be - fore an - y trou - ble got start - ed.

be - - fore an - y trou - ble got start - ed.

but the o - cean

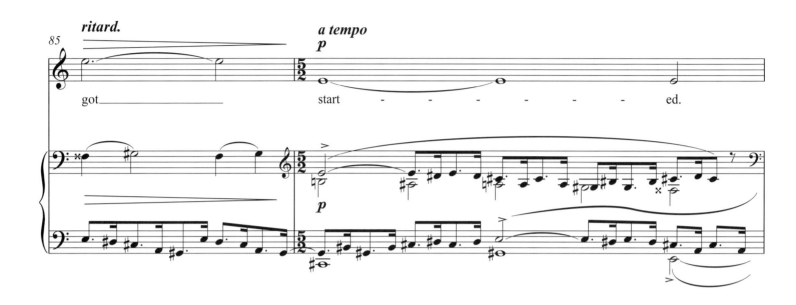

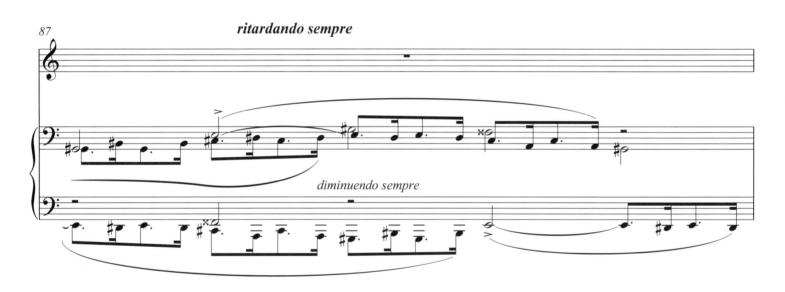

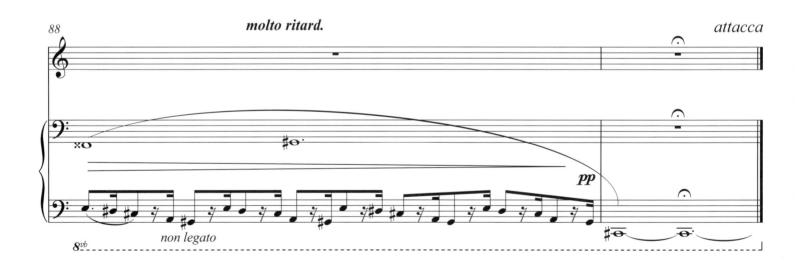

10/8/96
New York City

for Tobias Schneebaum and Joel Singer

III. A Few Romances

JOSHUA BECKMAN

DAVID DEL TREDICI

found___ out there were a lot___) ev - 'ry - thing went smooth as could be

due to the cour - tes - y and stealth of those young op - er - a - tors and al - though

con Pedale

things got back to nor - mal the next day — no re - flec - tion on you — more than a

few ro - man - ces bud - ded out of the sparks of that con -

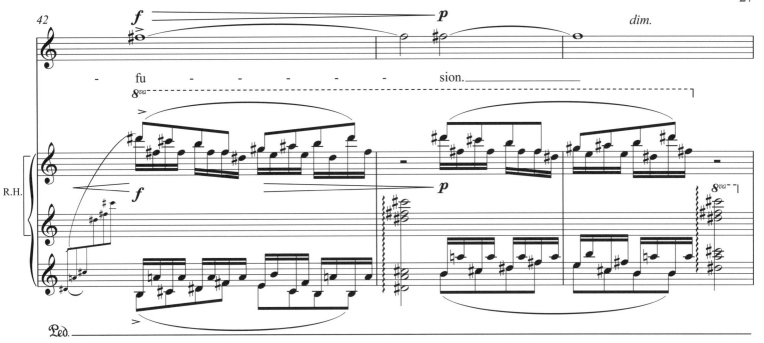

- fu - - - - - sion.

INTERLUDE:

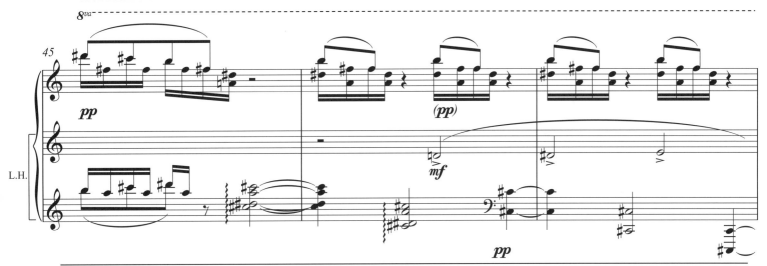

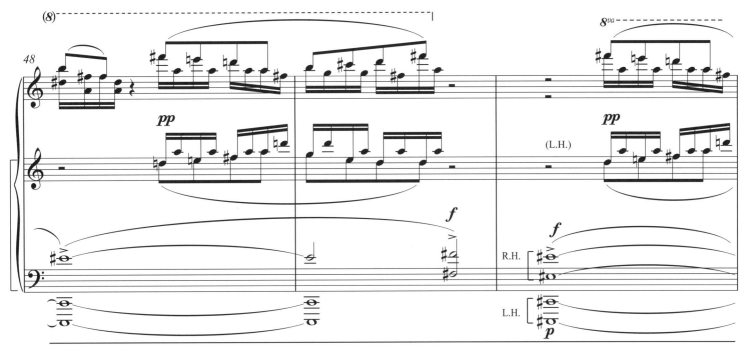

28

→ *no changes (al fine)* _____

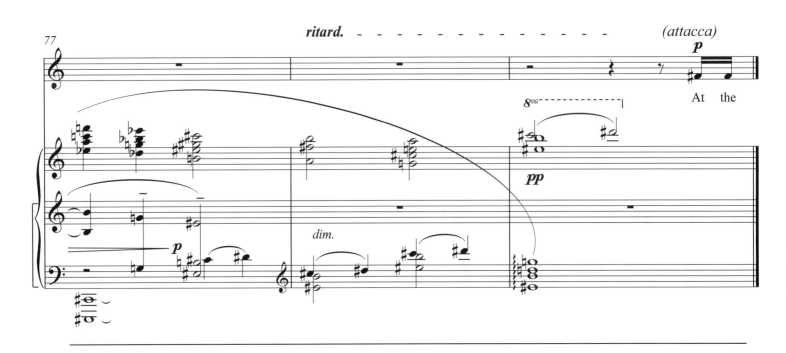

At the

M-051-93368-6

7/18/98, Yaddo

In memoriam: John Krams
IV. Walking

JOSHUA BECKMAN

DAVID DEL TREDICI

Andantino (♩ = 96)

news of your death cou-ples who had nev- er heard of you kept walk - ing

and were on - ly dragged back by the nag-ging sen - sa - tion that___

af - ter hun - dreds of miles they had___ left home and fam - 'lies un - at -

* no pedal change until measure 21

7/3/98, MacDowell Colony

M-051-93368-6

for John Corigliano

V. Rebellion

JOSHUA BECKMAN

DAVID DEL TREDICI

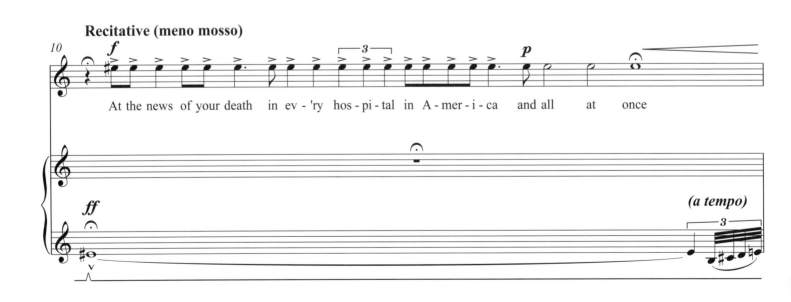

At the news of your death in ev - 'ry hos - pi - tal in A - mer - i - ca and all at once

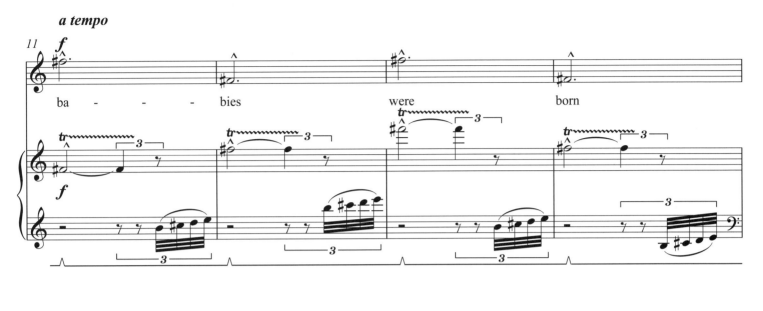

Dance of the riled children:

choc - 'late milk____ choc - 'late milk choc - 'late milk____ choc - 'late milk

and they threw____ their____ pa -

ja - mas out the win - dow

out____ the____ win - dow____

and snuck____ dir - ty books___ to bed

Viel schneller
(tempo primo, ♩ = 116)

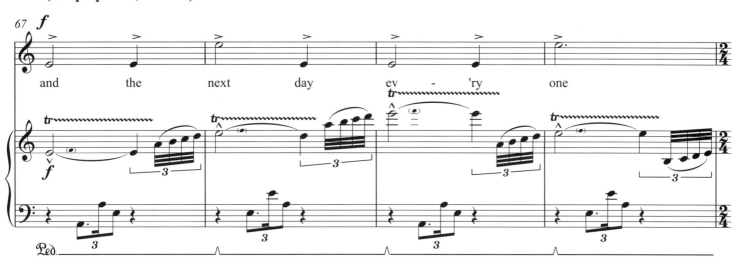

and the next day ev - 'ry one

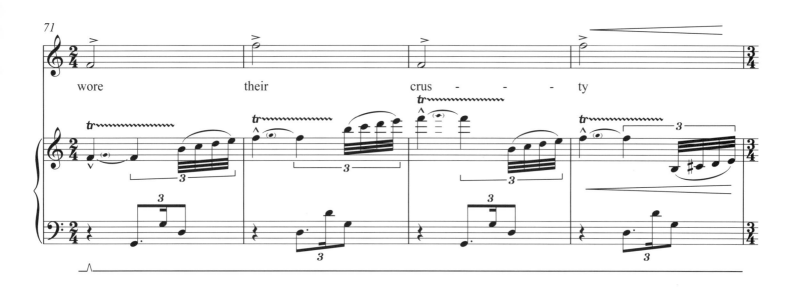

wore their crus - - ty

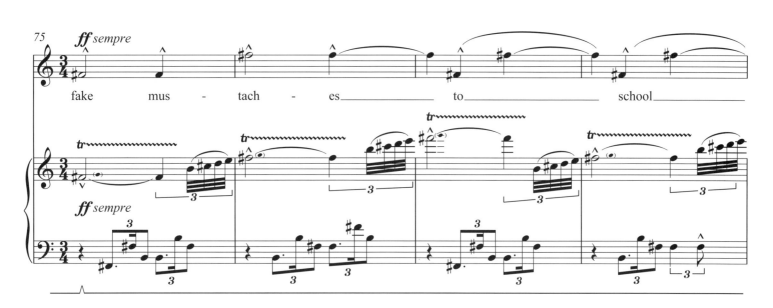

fake mus - tach - es to school

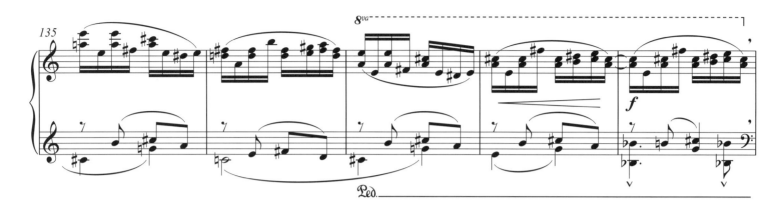

At the news of your death and all at once ba - bies were born and then slapped

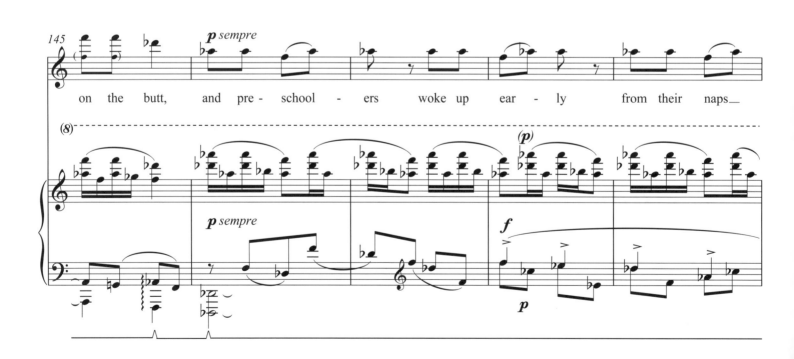

on the butt, and pre - school - ers woke up ear - ly from their naps__

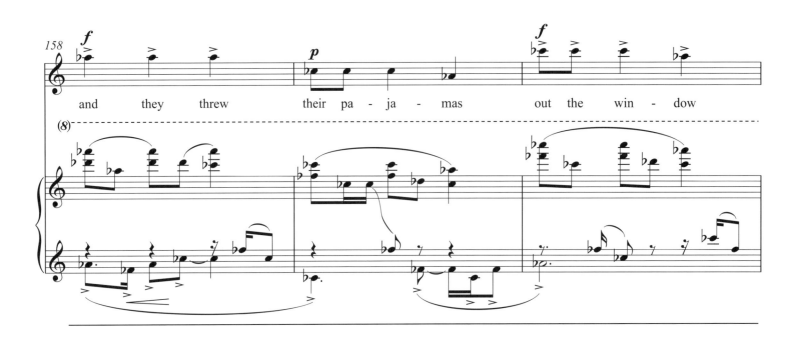

and they threw their pa - ja - mas out the win - dow

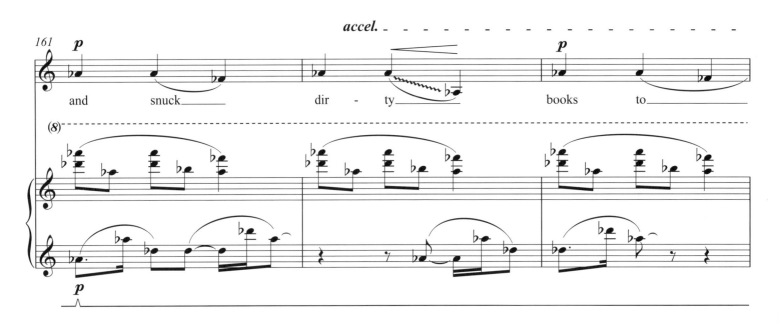

and snuck dir - ty books to

Schneller (♩ = 132)

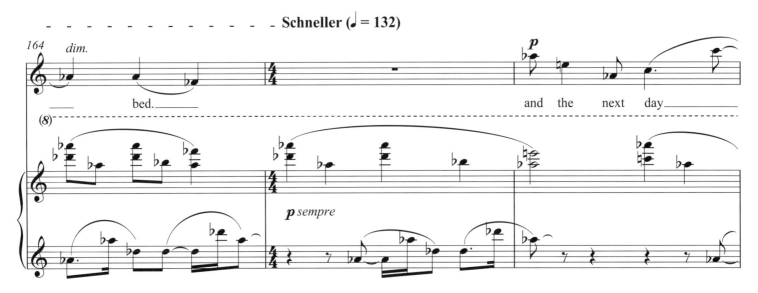

bed. and the next day

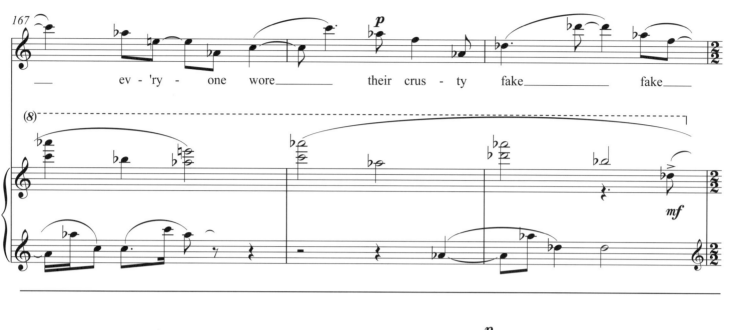

ev - 'ry - one wore_____ their crus - ty fake_____ fake_____

_____ mus - tach - es   to_____ to school_____

and an - swered their_____   teach - er's ques - - tions in_____

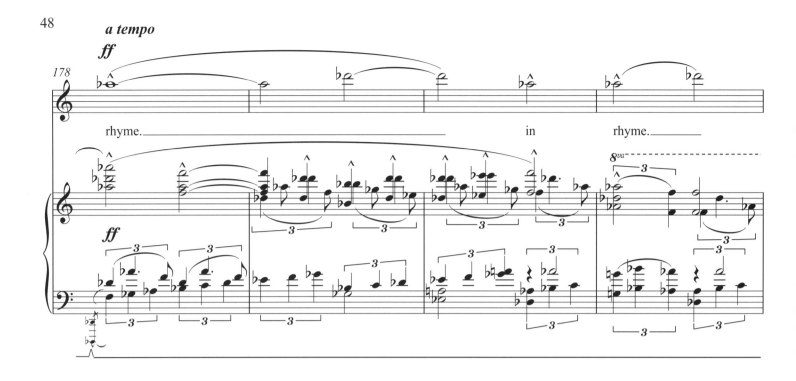

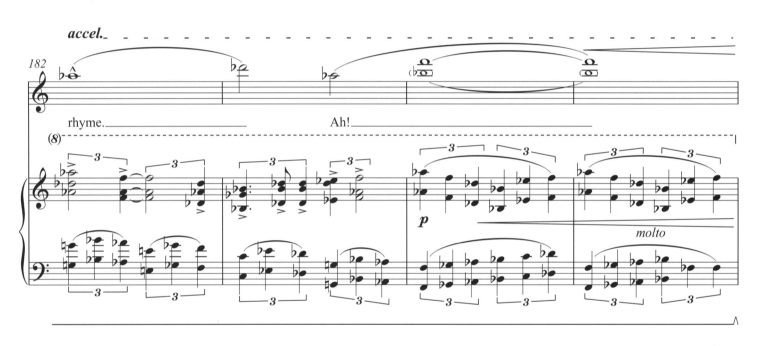

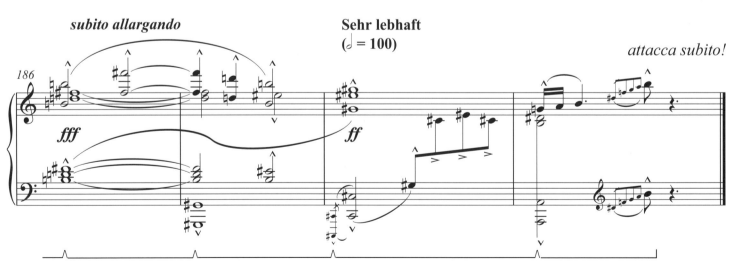

7/25/98, Yaddo

for Tom Cipullo
VI. A Good Cry

JOSHUA BECKMAN

DAVID DEL TREDICI

got up from their chairs, mis - ty,

think - ing_____ it

was their_____ wives_____ or_____ their age_____

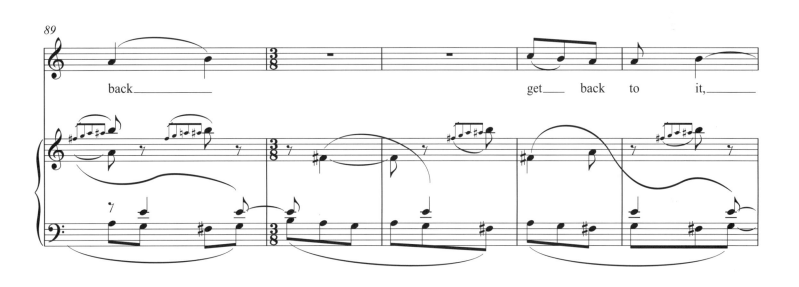

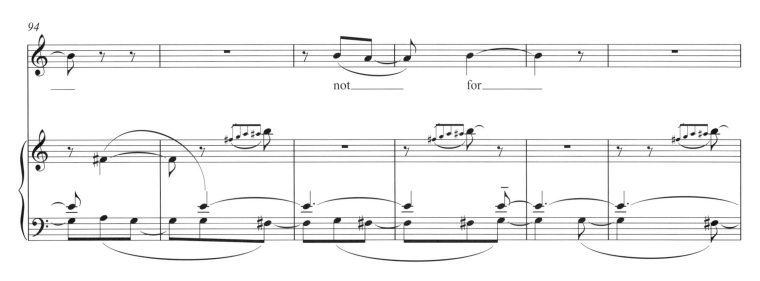

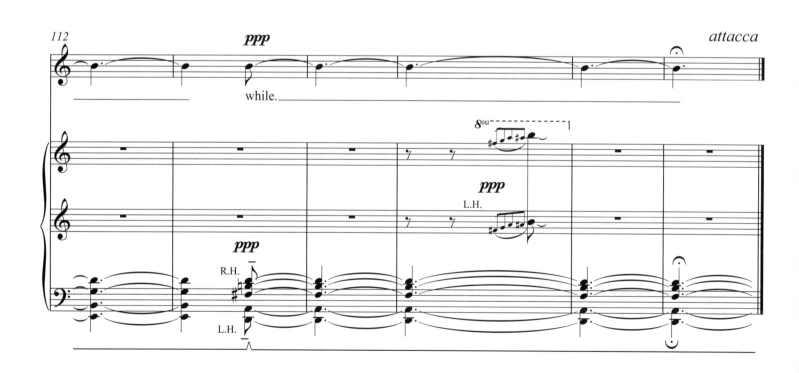

7/16/98, Yaddo

INTERLUDE:

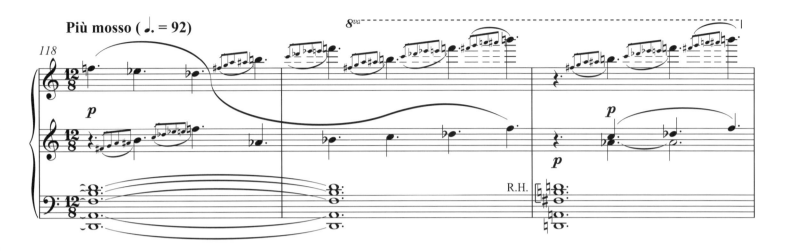

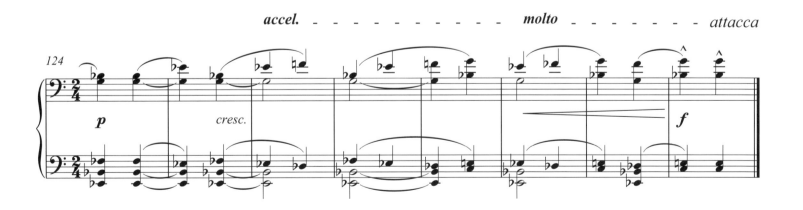

7/5/01
MacDowell Colony

for my brothers, Bobby, Richard and Peter

VII. A Point of Contention

JOSHUA BECKMAN

DAVID DEL TREDICI

Allegro maestoso (♩ = 120)

At the news of your death on the day

that you died the pa-per came with a lit-tle note say-ing that you were a

cra - zy and good man, which I knew and that you were a

ta - lent - ed po - et with thir - ty books to your cre - dit, which I knew

and say - ing

that you were dead,

so I went out and threw it in the

60

64

QUODLIBET:

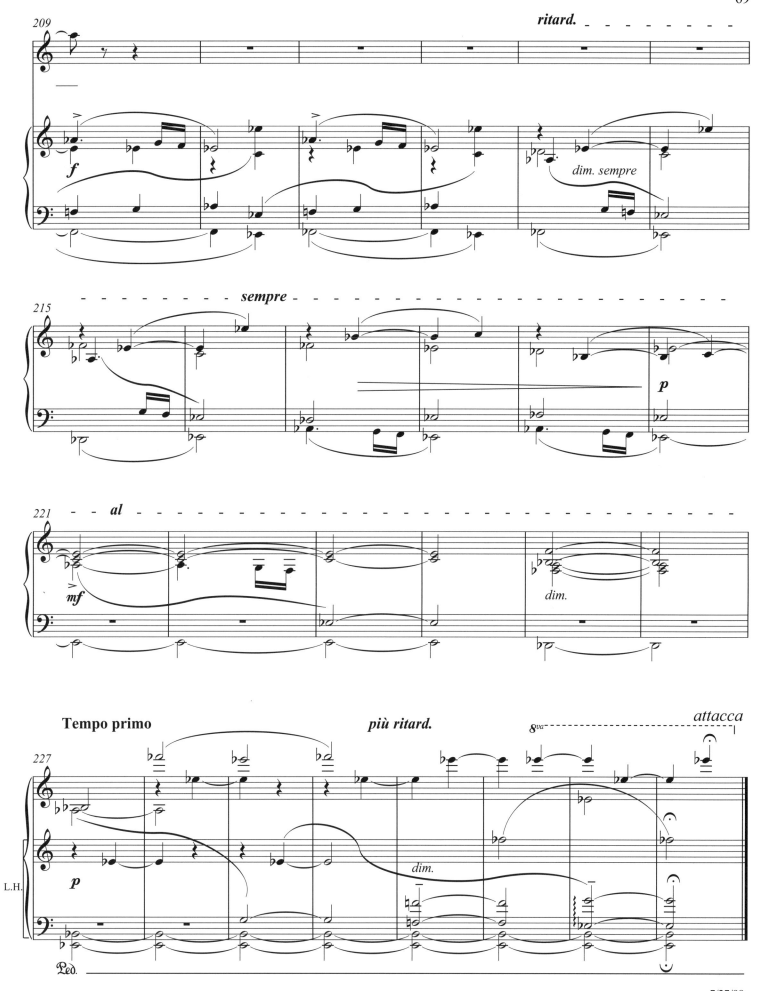

7/27/98
Yaddo

M-051-93368-6

for my sister, Ann
VIII. Sweeter

JOSHUA BECKMAN

DAVID DEL TREDICI

Slow and mysterious (♩ = 69)

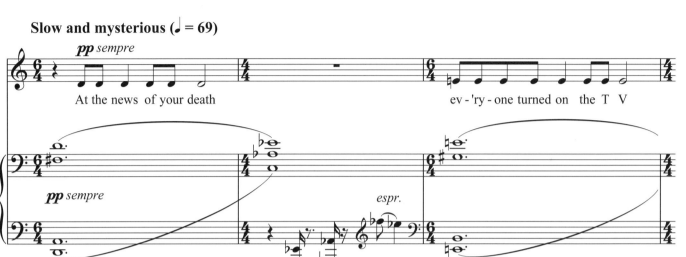

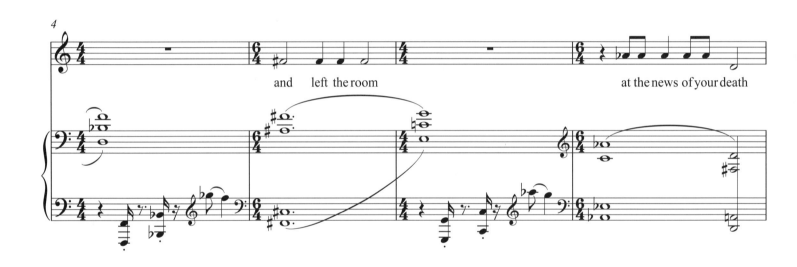

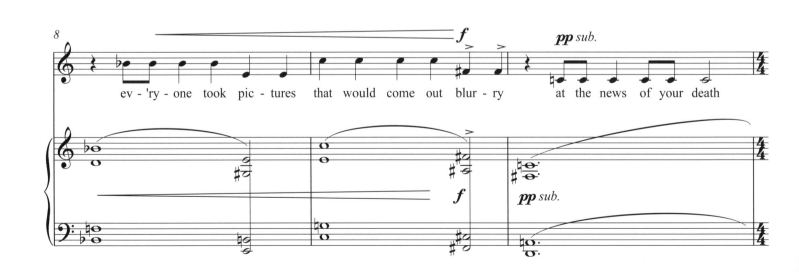

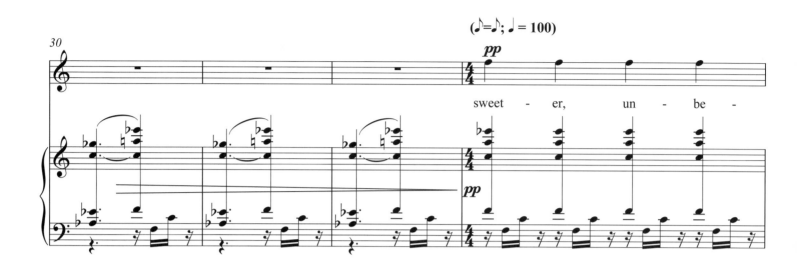

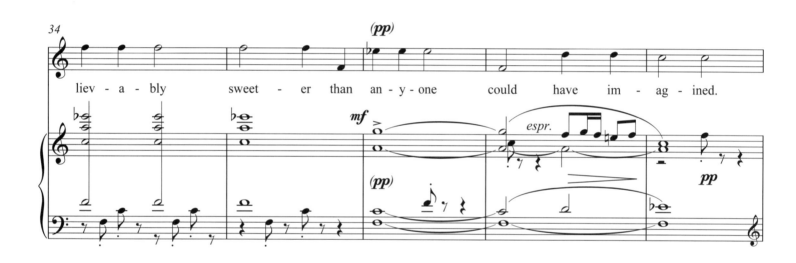

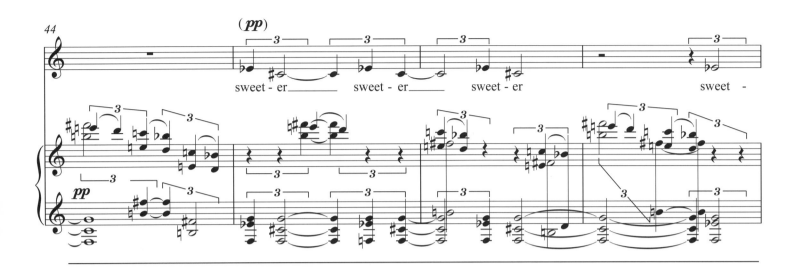

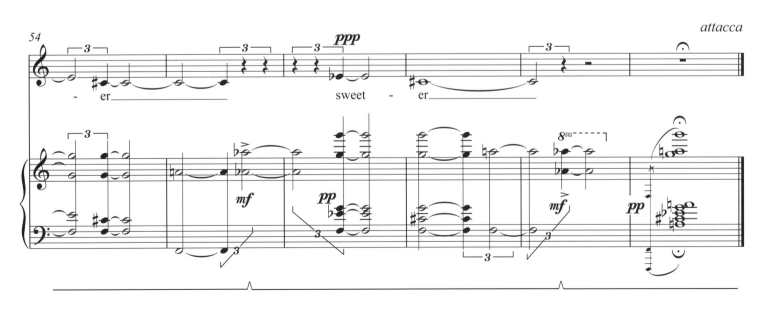

attacca

7/16/98
MacDowell Colony

M-051-93368-6

74

CADENZA:
Allegro con fuoco (♩ = 138)

(𝓟𝓮𝓭.) (no pedal changes until measure 31)

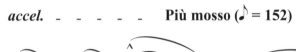

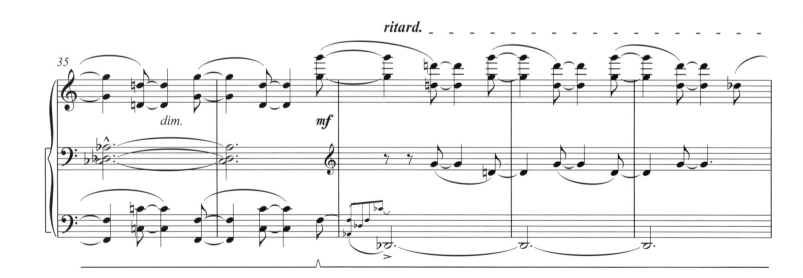

Meno mosso (♩. = 58)

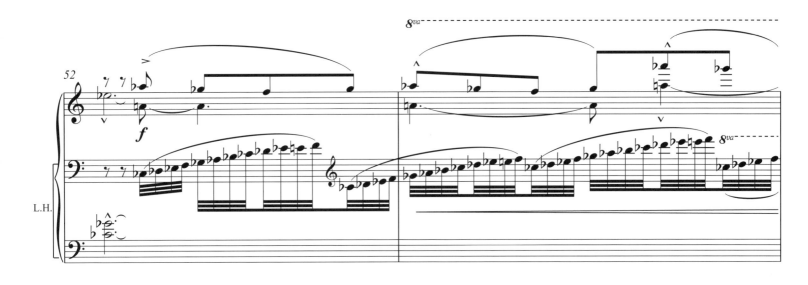

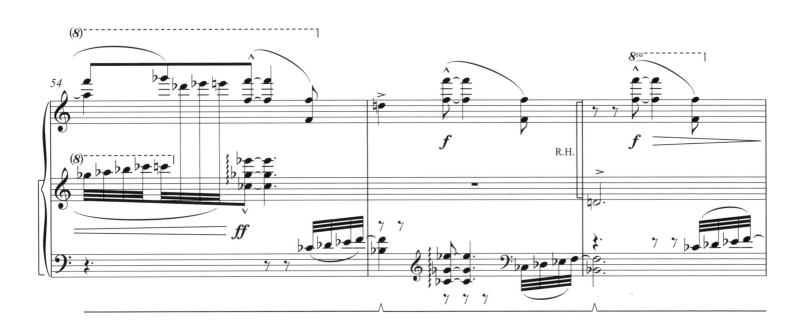

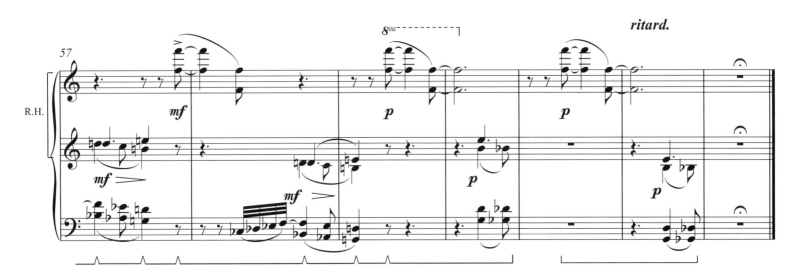

for myself

IX. David

JOSHUA BECKMAN

DAVID DEL TREDICI

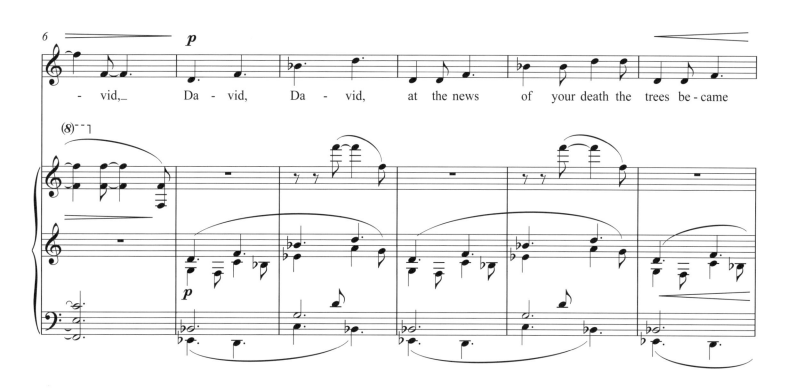

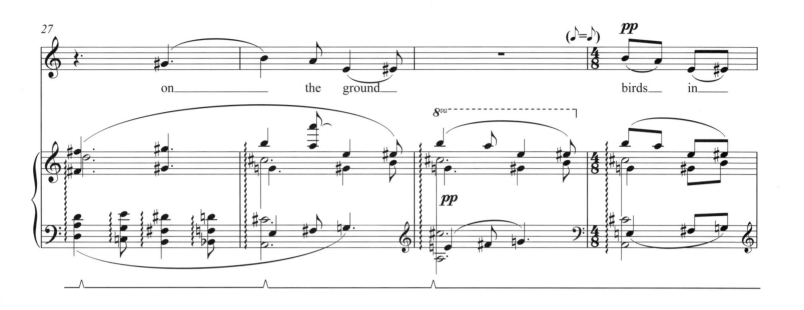

on _____ the ground _____ birds ___ in

na - ked ___ nests, and __ wind __ with no - thing to __ do __

all o - ver

più accel. _ _ _ _ _ _ _ _ _ _ _ _ _ _ _

stub - born and ig - no - rant ig - no - rant trees that they are_____

Ancora più mosso (♩. = 84)

they have pro - mised to_____ keep this_____ up_____ they have

pro - - - mised to keep_____ this up_____

N.B. Measures 64, 66, 68, 70: Accented notes, wherever they appear, must be clearly heard above the rest.

(no pedal change until measure 123)

they are de-ter-mined to keep this up Yes,

they are de-ter-mined to keep this up

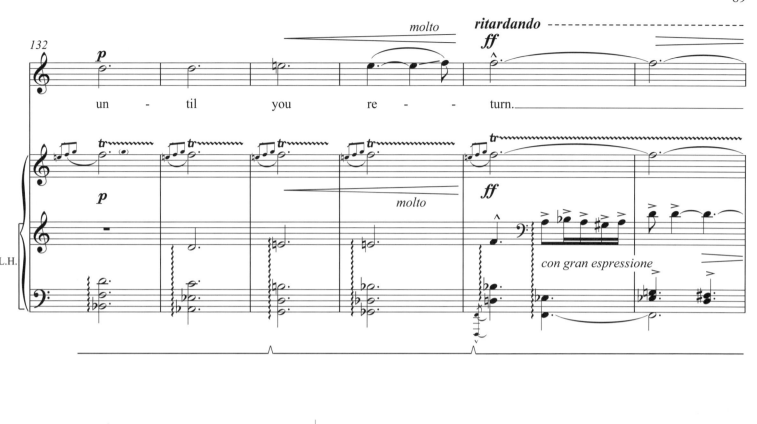

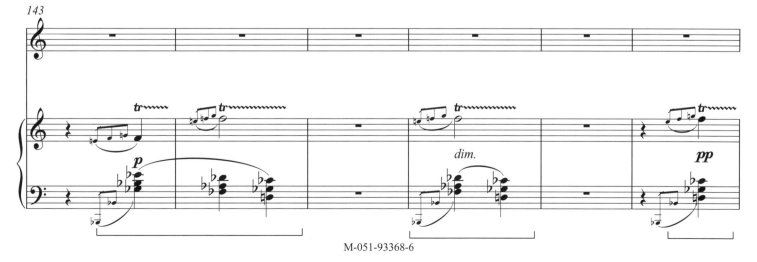

* During the four sung "Davids" which follow, the soprano must gradually move off stage, where the last "David" is sung.

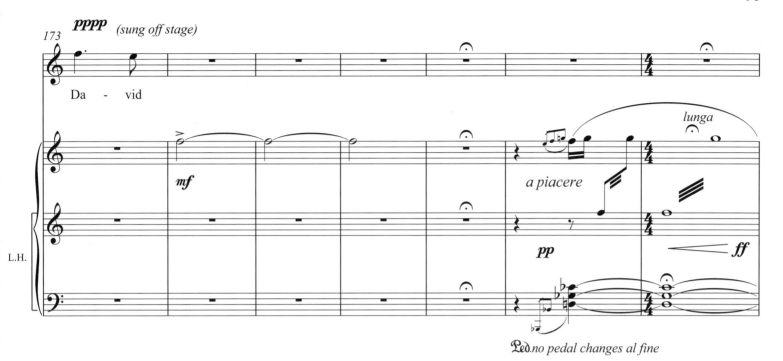

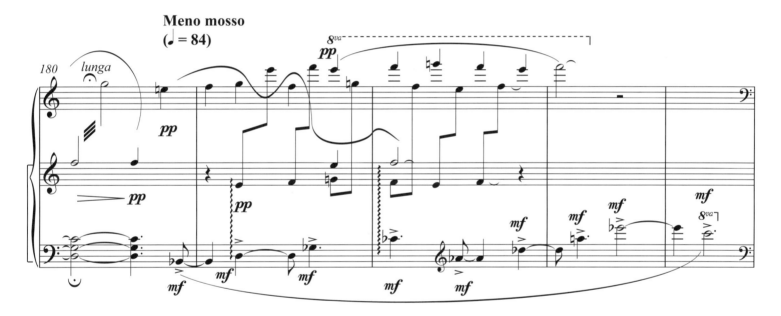

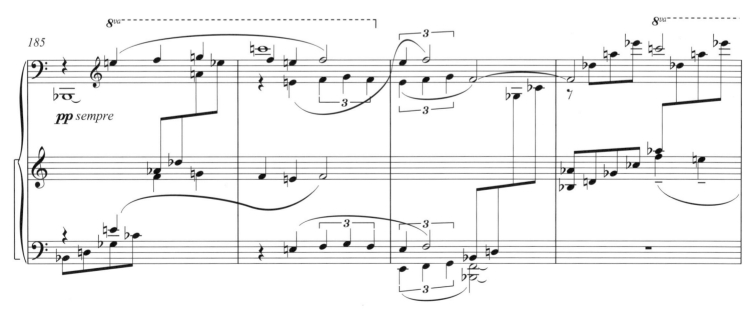

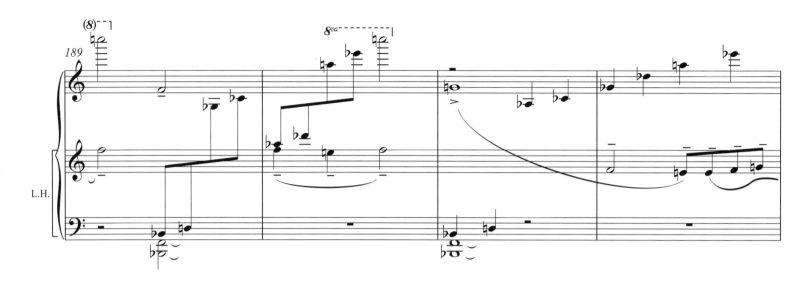

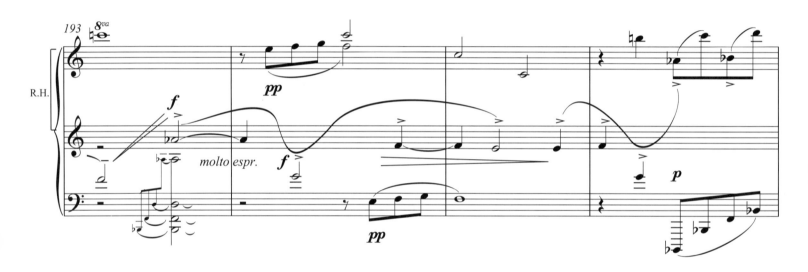

7/1/98 MacDowell Colony
Cycle written: 6/30-7/28/98
Revision/Expansion: 7/4 - 8/14/01

M-051-93368-6